SAN FRANCISCO BAY AREA

NATURE GUIDE and SAIJIKI

Edited by

Anne M. Homan
Patrick Gallagher
Patricia J. Machmiller

Published by the Yuki Teikei Haiku Society
Yuki Teikei Haiku Society, 6116 Dunn Avenue, San Jose, CA 95123

Copyright © Yuki Teikei Haiku Society, 2010

All rights reserved. No part of this book may be reproduced or transmitted in any form or by any means, electronic or mechanical, including photocopying, recording, or any information storage and retrieval system, without permission in writing from Yuki Teikei Haiku Society. The rights to the haiku in this volume are retained by the authors. The rights to the photographs and artwork are retained by the artists.

Second Edition
ISBN: 978-0-557-64551-0

Cover photo: Ed Grossmith

www.youngleaves.org

Acknowledgements

The descriptions of the natural world and local observances were written by the Saijiki Committee of the Yuki Teikei Society. Contributing members are:

    Roger Abe
    donnalynn chase
    D. Claire Gallagher
    Patrick Gallagher
    Anne M. Homan
    Patricia J. Machmiller
    Ebba Story

The first meeting of the Saijiki Committee was held in late 1999. Others involved in those early meetings which helped shape and focus the project include: Martha Dahlen, Hiroyuki Hiraoka, June Hopper Hymas, and Kiyoko Tokutomi. Along the way encouragement and counsel was given by Fay Aoyagi.

The Yuki Teikei Haiku Society is grateful to all the poets, photographers, and painters who contributed to this project. In particular we would like to thank Dick Finn and the Livermore Valley Camera Club for their contributions. Every effort has been made to obtain permission to use artwork and haiku in this publication.

What is a Saijiki?

A saijiki is a dictionary of seasonal elements used by haiku poets. It is also useful for naturalists and people interested in the natural history of an area. Each entry contains a description of the element including both its natural and its poetic qualities and is accompanied by haiku written as examples of its use as a poetic figure.

About the Yuki Teikei Saijiki Project

Traditional haiku includes a kigo or seasonal element, a word or phrase that connotes or denotes the season. The Yuki Teikei Haiku Society promotes the writing of haiku in English by encouraging writers to first learn the traditional haiku form. The quest for an English language saijiki started when Kiyoko Tokutomi first compiled the list of kigo for autumn and winter and published them in *Haiku Journal,* Vol.1, in 1977. In *Haiku Journal,* Vol. 2, 1978, Kiyoko published the list of kigo for spring and summer. In that same *Haiku Journal* Kiyoshi and Kiyoko Tokutomi wrote an article describing the saijiki and how it was used as a tool for haiku writers in Japan. In a letter to the membership dated 7 October 1978 they wrote:

> "Since the article about *saijiki* was printed in our most recent edition of *Haiku Journal,* many responses have been received encouraging us to begin compiling an English language *saijiki* . . . .
> "Over a period of years, we have been working on [it] in our spare time. And as many of you know, such an undertaking in addition to our regular activities would require many years before a compilation would be complete. We have been asked if such a project could be completed in a shorter period of time if we had a *Saijiki* Committee."

Kiyoshi and Kiyoko went on to call for volunteers to help with the development of material for an English language saijiki. Although many responded to their call for volunteers, the project proved to be too large for the young organization. After Kiyoshi died in 1987 the project became dormant.

Then in 1993 Patricia Machmiller and Kiyoko Tokutomi in a modest attempt to create an example of a saijiki published the *Monterey Bay and Peninsula Regional Saijiki* for participants' use at the annual Haiku Retreat at Asilomar in Pacific Grove CA. This saijiki used excerpts from various field guides of local flora and fauna and combined them with translations of traditional Japanese kigo that fit the region.

Finally in 1999 at the Haiku Retreat the idea surfaced once again of a regional saijiki for Yuki Teikei. A Saijiki Committee was once again formed, and eleven years later on the thirty-fifth anniversary of the Society, the *San Francisco Nature Guide and Saijiki,* a long-time dream of the Society's founders, became a reality.

Table of Contents

SPRING…..1
Landscape
    first blossoming tree…...2
    vernal pool…..3
Human Affairs
    César Chávez Day…..4
    Maverick Beach…..5
Animals
    by-the-wind sailor…..6
    gray fox…..7
    hilltopping…..8
    painted lady…..9
    returning gray whales…..10
    rookery…..11
    singing frogs…..12
    snowy plover…..13
    surfperch…..14
Plants
    California lilac; ceanothos…..15
    California poppy…..16
    Chinese houses…..17
    Douglas iris; mountain iris…..18
    field mustard…..19
    globe lily; fairy lantern…..20
    goldfields…...21
    Ithuriel's spear…..22
    madrone…..23
    manzanita…..24
    miner's lettuce…..25
    redwood sorrel…..26
    shooting star…..27
    sticky monkey flower…..28
    thrift…..29

SUMMER…..31
Landscape
    golden hills…..32
    summer fog…..33
    wildland fire…..34
Human Affairs
    Bay to Breakers Race…..35
Animals
    anise swallowtail…..36
    gopher snake…..37
    midshipman…..38
    smelt…..39
    water turtles…..40
Plants
    beach primrose…..41
    beach sagewort…..42
    coyote mint…..43
    elderberry…..44
    evening primrose…..45
    farewell-to-spring…..46
    hens-and-chickens, live-forever…..47
    matilija poppy…..48
    mariposa tulip…..49
    sand verbena…..50
    soap plant…..51
    tarweed…..52
    yellow star thistle…..53

AUTUMN…..55
Sky and Elements
    first rain….. 56
Landscape
    brown hills…..57
Human Affairs
    San Francisco Military
        Fleet Week…..58
Animals
    acorn woodpecker…..59
    California quail…..60
    migrating monarchs…..61
    migrating raptors…..62
    purple-striped jelly…..63
    tarantula…..64
Plants
    bigleaf maple…..65
    buckeye…..66
    buckwheat…..67
    clematis…..68
    huckleberry…..69
    oak apple, oak gall…..70
    pickleweed…..71
    rattlesnake grass…..72
    snowberry…..73
    ticking leaves…..74
    western hopbush…..75
    wild grape…..76

WINTER…..77
Sky and Elements
    cold rain…..78
Landscape
    arroyos come alive…..79
    kelp wrack…..80
    mudslides…..81
    snow on the peaks…..82
    tule fog…..83
Human Affairs
    Julia Morgan…..84
    olive harvest…..85
    John Steinbeck…..86
Animals
    California newt…..87
    elephant seal….88
    junco flocks…..89
    ladybug…..90
    northern harrier…..91
    sanderling…..92
    steelhead…..93
    white-crowned
        sparrow…..94
    yellow-billed magpie…..95
Plants
    artichoke…..96
    coyote brush…..97
    oak mistletoe…..98
    sycamore…...99
    toyon…..100

dedicated to
the memory of
D. Claire Gallagher

SPRING

LANDSCAPE

first blossoming tree

In California one of the very special moments of the year is the sighting of the first blossoming: It might be an acacia along the Santa Cruz highway, or a plum tree peeking over someone's back fence, or a tulip magnolia beside a dilapidated house in an old neighborhood. The first sighting is usually unexpected, for when it happens the skies are still overcast and if it is not raining, rain is in the forecast and there is still the threat of frost at night. It is when we are most deeply immersed in the mind of winter that we suddenly come upon a blossoming tree, and we are filled with elation and relief—elation that, indeed, there is renewal and relief that the dark time we are now in is almost ended.
pjm

first blossom—
asleep in his pram
the new baby
           Patricia Prime

passing an alley
the conversation ceases—
first plum blossoms
           pjm

Photos: Patrick Gallagher ("Poppies," previous page), Don Homan

vernal pool

Vernal pools fill with water during winter rains and slowly dry as the weather warms, the days grow longer, and the rains stop. In pools on rocky surfaces, tiny animals such as the fairy shrimp live out their short lives. In pools on soils, specialized wildflowers bloom. Some of these in the Bay Area are blue downingia (shown in photo), a lobelia relative; yellow glue-seed; bluish vernal pool mint with its refreshing fragrance. The flowers begin blooming when the water recedes as it evaporates, and thus are arranged in multicolored rings.

      The soil pools develop in clay on top of a hardpan layer. Fairy shrimp and many of the wildflowers associated with vernal pools are now endangered because vernal pools themselves are endangered. Ranchers and farmers plow over the little wetlands. Housing developments cover them with asphalt and cement. Most of the vernal pools in the Bay Area are gone.

amh/dcg

vernal pool
adrift on its surface
a few loose clouds
        Linda Robeck

vernal pool
  the shapes
of the past
        Michael Dylan Welch

fairy shrimp
darting through the vernal pool
staccato notes
        Anne M. Homan

holding
onto the moon
vernal pool
        Carolyn Thomas

Photo: John Game

HUMAN AFFAIRS

César Chávez Day

March 31, the day of César Chávez's birth in 1927 in Yuma, Arizona, is celebrated by California as a state holiday. Chávez was a farm worker of Mexican heritage who became a labor leader and civil rights activist. He co-founded the National Farm Workers Association, which became the United Farm Workers. Chávez first came to national attention with his involvement in the 1965 grape boycott to protest low wages for farm workers—the boycott lasted for five years. In 1969 Chávez and the UFW marched through the Imperial and Coachella valleys to the border of Mexico, protesting growers' use of illegal immigrants as strikebreakers. In the early '70s he helped to organize a boycott for lettuce workers. An advocate for nonviolent social change, he often fasted to call attention to labor problems that he felt needed to be addressed. During a 25-day fast in Phoenix in 1970, the famous phrase "Sí, se puede" (Yes, it can be done) first became the rallying cry for farm workers for fair wages and better working conditions. In 1988 he fasted for 36 days to protest the use of pesticides. Four years later he directed a march of more than 10,000 farm workers in the Salinas Valley.

César Chávez died on April 23, 1993 in Arizona. He received the U.S. Medal of Freedom from President Clinton posthumously and was inducted into the California Hall of Fame by Governor Arnold Schwarzenegger and First Lady Maria Shriver in 2006.
amh

César Chávez Day—
day workers on the curb
in front of Taco Bell
        Linda Papanicolaou

Maverick Beach

"If everybody had an ocean/across the U.S.A./ then everybody'd be surfin'/like Californ-I-A." In the Beach Boys days of the early 1960s, surfing became a fad on California beaches. Teenagers talked their parents or grandparents out of the old family Woodie station wagon, loaded it up with surfboards and picnic gear and headed for the waves. No one worried about skin cancer—the browner the better.

     Some years later, a rumor began making the rounds about a truly great surfing area north of Half Moon Bay. It probably remained a secret so long because it is accessible only by hiking two miles. The place is called Maverick Beach, or Mavericks, in honor of its wild and crazy rides. An average day yields 20- to 30-foot waves; on a really good day, the waves can be more than 50 feet. Dangerous holes and rocky outcrops make it one of the most dangerous surf breaks in the world. Legendary surfer Mark Foos died there. Today, surfers and event sponsors actually track the weather patterns on the Internet to determine big wave days. Mavericks is the first competition of the year on the U.S. West Coast, usually in February. There are four heats; best out of three takes the prize.
amh

waves swamp the press tent
at Maverick Beach
#@#! deleted
        Ann Bendixen

Mavericks
another surfboard
without a rider
        Garry Gay

Photo: John Lankes

ANIMALS

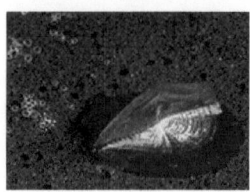

by-the-wind sailor
Velella velella

By-the-wind sailors are small jellyfish of a deep transparent blue that cluster together in large rafts. They are born in the Pacific Ocean over the mid-Pacific Ridge. Half of the new jellies have sails that tack to the left and half tack to the right, so they are blown both eastward and westward. Seen from a distance they appear to be large purple patches on the sea. If they come too close to shore, the high on-shore winds of March will beach them. The tide line is then covered with thousands of stranded by-the-wind sailors. Their deep blue bleaches in the sun and in a few days they become white, transparent, and paper-like, and are easily blown away on the wind.
pjm

the papery bits
of *velella velella*—
how fleeting this life
       pjm
       Blush of Winter Moon 2001

dusk—
is there a hierachy
in by-the-wind sailor nation
       Fay Aoyagi

by-the-wind-sailors
you to the east
I to the west
       Fay Aoyagi

Photo: Sherry Ballard © California Academy of Sciences

gray fox
Urocyon cineroargenteu

Late spring is the time for noticing foxes because their pups are born in April or May, and this forces the family to be more aggressive in its search for food. Mostly nocturnal in habit, native gray foxes are much shyer than their imported red cousins, and some biologists worry that the red fox is replacing the gray. The gray fox has shorter legs than the red fox, and this probably enables it to climb and use tree hollows for dens. It will also climb trees to search out bird nests to eat the eggs or the young. Foxes have a varied diet—berries and fungi as well as small rodents, birds, and insects. The gray fox has a silver coat, but its throat and belly show patches of reddish-gold, brown, and/or white. The gray fox does not have a white tip on its tail.
amh

I must admit
I do not frequent your haunts
gray fox
              June Hymas

monastery woods
gray fox and her kit
watching me watching them
              Joan Zimmerman

Photo: Gerald and Buff Corsi © California Academy of Sciences

hilltopping

"Hilltopping" is a mating behavior exhibited by many species of butterflies. Oakley Shields, who has studied this phenomenon, has shown that males fly in great numbers at the tops of hills and that unmated females come to the hilltops, mate, and then return to lower elevations. Swallowtails and western whites have been seen hilltopping, and J.W. Tilden has observed the anise swallowtail, the western tiger swallowtail, and the Colombian skipper in these nuptial flights on Mt. Hamilton near San Jose.
pjm

in looping spirals
the hilltopping butterflies—
Callas aria
        pjm

Mt. Hamilton's Eye
shuttered to the butterflies'
noontime hilltopping
        pjm

painted lady
Vanessa cadui

Flocks of painted lady butterflies come into the Bay Area in late spring on their migration from southern desert breeding grounds to northern summering fields. The species is sometimes called the thistle butterfly because of the caterpillars' food preference. The wingspan is from 1½ to 2 inches; the wing uppersides are black with white spots toward the tip and orange with black spots near the body. The four spots at the rear of each hind wing are totally black, distinguishing the painted lady from similar species. The individual butterflies that reach the Bay Area are likely to show fraying on the trailing edges after their arduous journey. This can be taken as a sign that the generative property of spring is nearly spent.
pg

dancing down the trail
staying just in front of us—
the painted lady
                   Carol Steele

returning gray whales
Eschrichtius robustus

On a clear day in spring, one may see from a coastal headland the plume of whale breath spray, or with luck, a breach of a gray whale leaping from the water, displaying its body and flipping its tail. Californians and visitors, by land, sea, and plane, turn out to view the slow-moving gray whale migration along the California coast as whales return from Baja to the feeding grounds in the Bering Sea and, north of that within the Arctic Circle, the Chukchi Sea.

     Mating behavior involving a pod of three adult whales—one supporting the female under water—is frequently observed. The northward migration with the new calves is a sure sign of spring. The chance of better weather and the presence of such large babies may be what make whale watching so rewarding in March and April.
dcg

returning whale—
lending our binoculars
to foreign tourists
          D. Claire Gallagher

Gray whale migration
 several plumes are seen . . .
one spy-hopping
          Garry Gay

is there a God
or is there no God
returning gray whales
          Anne M. Homan
            YTHS anthology 2002

returning gray whales
one plume, then another
salt-stained eyeglasses
          Elaine and Neal Whitman

Photo: Marilyn Russell

rookery, heronry

Heron and egret rookeries exist around the Bay Area, usually close to tidal areas, but most of them are inaccessible. Audubon Canyon Ranch is a private nature preserve overlooking Bolinas Lagoon that is open to the public on weekends from mid-March to mid-July. Male great blue herons arrive here in early February, and male great egrets and snowy egrets in mid-March. The male birds claim their territory and start to build large platform nests of sticks lined with finer twigs and plant material. Soon the females arrive, and the males begin their courtship behavior of bowing, stretching, and spreading their decorative feathers. Visitors can walk up into the canyon and sit on wooden benches at a hillside overlook to observe the birds. This close-up view of the rookery across the canyon in the tops of old redwood trees is amazing. After the eggs hatch, the adults feed the hungry chicks from food caught in the lagoon. In May, most of the young birds learn to fly.
      Another well-known rookery is at Elkhorn Slough near Moss Landing.
amh

Bolinas town
heron nestlings high above
the aging hippies
          Patrick Gallagher

egret rookery
a sudden silence brings me
up from the eyepiece
          Anne M. Homan

the cloud armada
blows steadily inland …
rookery feathers
          Anne M. Homan
          YTHS 2009 Anthology

Artist: Floy Zittin

singing frogs

People unfamiliar with the nightly chorus of singing Pacific tree frogs in spring often mistake it for the sound of crickets. One San Jose household with a small pond had such a large population of tree frogs that the neighbors complained to the local authorities about their loud singing. This little native frog, three-fourths to two inches long, occurs in various colors: green, gray, brown, tan. It can change from dark to light color in a few minutes; often it has dark spots on its back and legs. It has black eyestripes and toepads. Although it can climb well, it usually stays close to the ground, eating mostly insects. Typically, its voice is a loud "kreck-ek" with a rising inflection.

The frog chorus sometimes includes the much larger bullfrog. Those who don't recognize its booming voice would swear that there must be some strange large beast, possibly pig-sized, close by.

Some nights the endangered red-legged frog (see photo), the frog in the original jumping frog contest, joins in the singing.
ra/dc

soundless footsteps
abruptly they quiet
the singing frogs
        Anne M. Homan
            YTHS anthology 2001

singing frogs
even they can't bring a smile
to Tiger Woods
        Patrick Gallagher

moon set
the closeness
of the frog chorus
        Laurabell

Frog chorus—
you would never know
if they sang off key
        Garry Gay

Photo: Scott Hein (www.heinphoto.com)

snowy plover
Charadrius alexandrius

This small pale plover lays its three spotted buff-colored eggs on a scrap of sand on the dunes anywhere along the Pacific Coast from southern Washington south to Baja. For this reason it is an endangered species. (Other shore birds have the good sense to nest in the Arctic where they are left more or less alone.)

    The snowy plover nests from mid-March to mid-August. The parents take turns sitting on the nest. Their sand-colored backs blend easily into their sandy surroundings. They have one incomplete breastband and a white hindneck collar. While it is difficult to distinguish them from sanderlings in their winter plumage, they are a bit smaller than sanderlings. Plovers are also more often seen alone or in pairs—sanderlings seem to gather in crowds.

    The snowy plover got its name not because of snow, but because it is lighter in color than the plover of Japan.

pjm

snowy plovers—
rivulets run through
the washed-out sand castle
                    pjm

Photo: Robert Harrington

surfperch
Amphistichus ssp.

Surf perches are members of the family of viviparous perches that frequent the sandy surf. The body is compressed and elliptical in outline, up to about 17 inches long and weighing between two and four pounds at maturity. During spring and early summer, the females give birth to 8 to 45 perfect miniatures of the parents, except the young have proportionately larger fins and brighter colors. Their diet consists of sandcrabs and small fish.

The barred surfperch is the most common species in the San Francisco Bay Area; its range is between Mexico and Bodega Bay. It has pronounced greenish to brown vertical bars across the body alternating with rows of spots of the same color, with a brassy coloring between the markings. The sides and belly are silvery gray.

Surfperch are gamefish prized by surf fishers. This type of fishing is a solitary occupation that requires patient waiting on the beach and an expert reading of the waves. Surf fishers can use bait or lures. As a rule, they are tight-lipped about their favorite bait, lure, and "hot spots."
ra

the angler casts
into an onshore breeze—
surfperch
                Linda Papanicolaou

Photo: Shiner surf perch courtesy of the Monterey Bay Aquarium

PLANTS

California lilac; ceanothus
Ceanothus spp.

Ceanothus has more species in California than any other native genus except perhaps manzanita. Blooms range from deep-reddish blue through pale blue to white. So many species to brighten spring! The taller blue-bloomers are known collectively as California lilac. One of the most common local species is blue blossom, *Ceanothus thyrsiflorus*, which blooms March through May in moist wooded hills.

Others are found in chaparral, mixed evergreen forest, meadows, oak woodland, and redwood forests. Besides varying in habitat, ceanothus also varies widely in size, from woody recumbent ground covers to small trees. All bear fragrant flower clusters composed of tiny individual flowers amid thick green leaves. Plants in the wild are frequently shaped by browsing deer, coast winds, or other environmental forces. It is common to see many ceanothus plants in proximity bluing natural areas; ceanothus has also become a popular landscaping plant.

Blossoms of ceanothus rubbed vigorously with water yield a fragrant soap. It is reported that part of a marriage ceremony for some Native Americans included the bride and groom washing each other's hair with ceanothus blossoms. Other uses included flower and leaf tea, tobacco, dye from the roots, stems for basketry, and a tonic made from the bark. dcg

all the way
to the blue-sky moon—
scent of ceanothus
                D. Claire Gallagher

Photo: Patrick Gallagher

poppy, California
Eschscholzia californica

The California poppy grows not only along coastal bluffs—so visibly ablaze for the early mariners—but also throughout most foothills of both coast and inland ranges. It was an excellent choice for the California state flower.

This short-lived perennial springs from a long taproot. The cluster of feathery, fern-like leaves is bluish-green. Blooms appear as early as March and continue well into summer depending on moisture. Early in the season flowers are large, strikingly orange, even reddish orange, and nearly as deep as tulips. Later blooms are smaller, shallower, and often a pale yellow or yellowish orange.

Like many poppy species, California poppy contains some opiate-type alkaloid. Wintu and Yuki people put a bit of the fresh root into the cavity of an aching tooth. Rumsien Ohlone parents placed several flowers underneath a young one's bed for quiet sleep!
dcg

---

filled with the sunbeams,
swaying in the gentle breeze—
the cups of poppies
        Kiyoshi Tokutomi

morning sun
filling the east-facing windows
poppies
        D. Claire Gallagher

poppy orange
it goes
with everything
        Patrick Gallagher

late-blooming poppies
their growth stunted by grass—
he's been dead one year
        pjm
        Blush of Winter Moon

first poppy
in the fallow field . . .
evening light
        Carolyn Thomas

Photo: Don Homan

Chinese houses
Collinsia heterophylla

The plant Chinese houses, also known as blue-eyed Mary, has flowers with whorls arranged on the stem in tiers, so the arrangement somewhat resembles a tiered Chinese pagoda. The showy blooms are like miniature snapdragons, with a pale pink upper lip and a lower lip of magenta. Chinese houses can spread in wide swaths over an open wooded hillside in lightly shaded areas. The stems are about six to eight inches in length. The plants bloom in April, before the fairy lanterns and mariposas, but after the shooting stars. amh

the sweetness
of the canyon shade—
blue-eyed Mary
        Linda Papanicolaou

Wooded hillside
she skips with her basket
through Chinese houses
        Garry Gay

Photo: Rebecca Davies

Douglas iris/mountain iris
Iris douglasiana

The Douglas iris is an enduring plant, blooming from February (even January in warm coastal pockets) into early summer. The lance leaves of its typical iris shape remain glossy through summer drought and winter cold. It grows from woody rhizomes in shallow spokes outward from the center to form colonies in open woodland, grassland, and the west slopes of coastal bluffs. The leaves are poisonous as food. Grazing and browsing animals learn to leave them alone.

    The elaborate flowers are borne on foot-high stalks. In Greek mythology, Iris was the goddess of the rainbow. The name is apt for a species that presents itself in a variety of colors that seem related to the environment. Near the coast the blooms are usually a deep, intense blue-purple; inland the shades are more delicate—lavender, cream, striped yellow, pale blue, pinkish white, or, rarely, pure white.

    The leaves contain long, fine, translucent fibers that Native Americans removed and rolled into high-quality twine, used for gathering bags, deer snare ropes, rabbit nets, and fishing nets of great size.
dcg

his smile approaching—
wind ripples the green lances
of mountain iris
                D. Claire Gallagher

three generations climb
up to the old silver mine—
the Douglas iris
                Carol Steele

Photo: Patrick Gallagher

field mustard
Brassica campestris

An old story claims that as the Catholic priests created new missions in California from San Diego northward, they dropped mustard seed so they could always follow the golden trail of spring blooms back to Mexico, just as Hansel and Gretel dropped bread crumbs to find their way home in the fairy tale. The true story of the introduction of non-native field mustard here is less romantic. Some of the tiny seed was mixed in livestock feed brought north from Mexico with mission supply expeditions. Later, mustard seed was knowingly imported for a cover crop in orchards and vineyards.

      Today in the Bay Area, in spring soon after the grass has turned green from winter rains, tiny mustard flowers yellow the hills and orchards in a brilliant spectacle. Full of nectar, the flowers are attractive to early spring bees. Field mustard is distinguishable from other mustards because its leaves clasp the stem of the plant. The lower leaves are pinnate and the upper leaves an arrowhead shape. The elongated seedpods are rounded. As the plant grows taller, sometimes as much as four feet, the leaves and yellow blossoms become less dense, and the stems create an untidy miniature forest.

amh

evening on the road
the scent of a mustard field
carried on the wind
           Patricia Prime

uprooted cherry trees—
between the bulldozer tracks
wild mustard blooms
           D. Claire Gallagher

wayside blooming
mayweed and scraggly mustard
along the barbed wire
           Anne M. Homan

her old CD
on the long drive
wild mustard
           Deborah P. Kolodji
           Daily Haiku, June 2010

Photo: Don Homan

globe lily/fairy lantern
Calochortus albus

The globe lily is inconspicuous until it blooms, on a grass-like stem from a basal group of two to six long leaves. Then in April or May, when your eye finds one in a shady glen or on a dry hillside, usually another and another will become visible as if by magic. Both buds and blossoms droop gracefully from the slender stems; the white petals, sometimes tinged with pale pink, curve toward each other, forming a dainty globe. This is one of the most winsome of spring flowers—one of the most prized. The petals keep a closed shape, never really opening. Tiny insects must crawl in deep to access the nectar, depositing pollen on hairs at the petal edges. On the slopes of Mount Diablo and in the North Bay, closely related species are lemon yellow in color.

    The plant's nutritious perennial bulbs were cooked and eaten by California Indians or dried and ground into flour. Loss of habitat now makes them uncommon and even more special.
dcg

barely pink
on the toe of a landslide…
fairy lantern
> D. Claire Gallagher

globe lilies
so modest there's no thought
of peeking in
> Patrick Gallagher

globe lily blossoms
we hear the neighing
of ghost horses
> Patrick Gallagher

new trail
bends round
the globe lily
> Joan Zimmerman

my fragile thoughts
protected from the rain
by a globe lily
> Roger Abe

Photo: Patrick Gallagher

goldfields
Lasthenia spp.

Goldfields are tiny yellow daisy-like flowers that bloom in abundance in open fields in March and April. In many locations large patches of goldfields combine with others to form multicolor carpets of great beauty. These displays are often found on soils high in serpentine, a green mineral originally formed under the sea. Serpentine outcrops are common in the San Francisco Bay coastal ranges. The mineral's composition inhibits the growth of many species of flora that would otherwise compete with or shade out the low-growing goldfields and their companions.
pg

past that moment when
the whole world did your bidding—
goldfields

                    pjm
                    YT Members' Anthology, 2009

Photo: Patrick Gallagher

Ithuriel's spear
Tritelaia laxa

Ithuriel's spear blooms in open woodlands or grasslands in the Bay Area. Very abundant in years of heavy rain, the funnel-shaped flowers vary in color from deep purple blue to sky blue. One genus, *Tritelaia hyacinthine*, found in wetter ground, is white. From April through June, the umbels splash open from leafless stems in hillside grasses, growing one to four feet in height. The leaves are iris-like lances with parallel veins.

Ithuriel was a good angel in *Paradise Lost* who was armed with a special spear that could pierce disguises. When Ithuriel lightly touched a toad near the sleeping Eve with his spear, the toad transformed into the fallen angel, Satan.

Native Americans cooked or ate raw the plant's edible corms, which the women pried from the hillsides with their digging tools. Perhaps some learned California pioneer, amazed at the transformation of a flower into a "potato," gave it its English name.
amh

Photo: Anne M. Homan

madrone
Arbutus menziesii

The showy Pacific madrone is a broadleaf flowering evergreen. This sturdy tree grows from 20 to 80 feet high in upland slopes and canyons. It has a stout, irregular crown of smooth red-orange branches. Its individual shiny dark leaves turn red before falling at any time of year. The thin bark on the trunk progresses from yellow-green to reddish brown before it darkens and is shed in shaggy strips to begin another cycle of color and renewal. The peeled trunk is cool and smooth and readily reveals all deep trauma. Both trunk and limbs are spreading and erratic—often shaped by their reach toward the sun under a canopy of conifers or mature oaks.

In early spring the red branches bear small urn-shaped white to pinkish flowers. In late spring the flowers litter wooded trails as if the Tooth Fairy has spilled her basket. Pale new growth of the Pacific madrone is from a distance startlingly like a dramatically blossoming tree.

Fall brings the maturing of warty buff-red berries, variable in their degree of tastiness and full of tiny seeds. They do not cling long to the tree.
dcg

so gently into
the swaying baby carriage
    madrone blossoms
        D. Claire Gallagher

madroño
beneath the white blossoms
a cold heart
        Patrick Gallagher

a half moon
behind the storm-split madrone—
she's half angry
        D. Claire Gallagher

evening breeze—
madrone blossoms shiver
on branches of sunset
        D. Claire Gallagher

Photo: Patrick Gallagher

manzanita

Arctostaphylos spp.

    The manzanita's droopy clusters of little creamy-pink urn-shaped blooms first appear in early spring, sometimes as early as mid-January. At this time, honeybees are not around, so the early blossoms' nectar is collected in daylight hours by bumblebees and hummingbirds and in the early evening by moths. The flower does not have a detectable odor. There are more than 50 species of manzanita in California. Although usually classified as a shrub, it often becomes a small tree, up to about 20 feet high. The largest local example, a bigberry manzanita in Sunol Regional Park, stands 33 feet. Still other species creep along the ground. Manzanita bark is a smooth dark red, but some of it dies and becomes a rough gray; often the two colors intertwine on the same plant. In late summer the red bark exfoliates, making little curls. Two species in our area are very rare: the raven manzanita in the Presidio and the Mt. Diablo manzanita.

    The name is Spanish for "little apple," referring to the red berries, which were ground and made into cider by Native Americans in what is now California. The generic name, *Arctostaphylos*, means "bear berries;" since they were one of the favored foods of our native grizzly, once the only bear in the Bay Area and now long gone from California overall. Today, deer, foxes, coyotes, skunks, and many birds feed on the fruit. With its oval-shaped leathery evergreen leaves, the plant is tolerant of drought and is a mainstay of the chaparral community, regenerating quickly after a wildfire. Native Americans burned the wood at dances and ceremonials because it burns with an unusually bright light.
amh

Photos: Anne M. Homan, Rebecca Davies, Anne M. Homan

miner's lettuce
Claytonia perfoliata

Common in moist wooded areas, this ubiquitous little charmer can even be found growing in crevices of tree trunks. The miniature white bouquet opening above the round perfoliate leaf is one of our early bloomers. Look for it from February through May. This dainty plant has three types of leaves: a narrow basal leaf, a paddle-like leaf, and the round perfoliate leaf supporting the tiny five-petaled flowers.

The fleshy leaves are tender and favored in salad or as cooked greens. Their high vitamin C content makes them a health food. Early sailors along the California coast reportedly came ashore to collect the plant for shipboard consumption to prevent scurvy, a disease common at sea because of lack of vitamin C. California Indians near the gold country laid leaves of miner's lettuce near red-ant hills. Ants crawling over the leaves left a vinegary trail of formic acid—salad with vinaigrette! Indians also made a laxative tea from the leaves. dcg

single file
through miner's lettuce—
the clasp of his hand
        Ebba Story

open gate—
goat kids and I
in the miner's lettuce
        Ebba Story

under the scrubs
the clumps of miner's lettuce
dressed in bird droppings
        Carolyn Fitz

filtered sunbeams
she whispers a secret
to the miner's lettuce
        Ebba Story

left to itself
this narrow-gauge railroad bed—
miner's lettuce
        pjm

Photo: Phyllis Lasche

redwood sorrel
Oxalis oregano

Patches of attractive white, rose-pink, or lavender flowers create lush floral mats in costal redwood and mixed evergreen forests in early spring and summer. The blooms turn from white to pink with age; the effect of a simultaneous variety of blossom hues gives a magical charm to the deeply shaded understory. Each three- to seven-inch flower stalk bears a solitary funnel-shaped bloom. The leaves are clover-like, with three heart-shaped leaflets. Often the leaf has a pale blotch in the center. Redwood sorrel leaves are extremely sensitive to the sun, folding down like umbrellas on hot days and at night.

The leaves and stems can be eaten raw in salads. The botanical name "oxalis" is derived from a Greek word meaning "bitter" or "sharp." The pioneers made a pie with these stems, which tasted much like rhubarb.
dcg

tripping down the path
a patch of redwood sorrel
catches then rights me
        donnalynn chase

forest twilight
redwood sorrel blossoms
catch all the light
        Patrick Gallagher

Photo: Gerald and Buff Corsi © California Academy of Sciences

shooting star
Dodecatheon hendersonii

The delicate shooting star is related to the cyclamen. This is noticeable in the flower, which looks as if a strong wind were constantly blowing the pinkish-purple petals backward. The end of the flower is capped by fused, pointed stamens so that it does resemble a shooting star. The oval-shaped leaves are basal, forming a mat after the winter rains, usually in open woodlands. Then the naked reddish stalks with flowering umbels shoot up in early spring to about one foot high or less.
amh

worried I hurry
down the path—am I too late
for the shooting stars?
                Anne M. Homan

Photo: Anne M. Homan

sticky monkey flower
Diplacus [Mimulus] aurantiacus

This evergreen two- to four-foot bush has three-inch deep green, glossy oval-shaped leaves and multi-branched stems. The flowers are arranged in whorls and are usually bright orange-yellow, yet can vary in color from a light cream to a deep orange. The five petals of each flower are arranged in two lips (an upper lip of two petals and a lower lip of three); all of these petals unite almost immediately into a long tube around the ovary. Slightly projecting from th tube, the cleft stigma has a tiny two-lobed tip; if touched on an unfertilized flower, the two lobes will come together in a slow "kiss." The sticky monkey flower blooms in late spring on dry slopes from California to Baja, a familiar showy shrub in the chaparral community. On hot days the leaves produce a sticky varnish to prevent water loss. Photo shows sticky monkey flower with lupine.
dc

forgotten lover
called into memory—
sticky monkey flower
        donnalynn chase

Photo: Margo Bors

thrift
America maritima var. *californica*

The California variety of thrift, a small one-half to one-inch globe of rose-pink to purple bracts, blooms on a naked stem that rises three to 15 inches from a tufted mound of grass-like green. The entire plant looks very much like a living pincushion. The blossom itself resembles a miniature onion flower. Thrift blooms from March to August along California's coastal bluffs and beaches.
pjm

the sting
of windborne sand—
sea thrift
        Linda Papanicolaou

Photo: Gerald and Buff Corsi © California Academy of Sciences

SUMMER

LANDSCAPE

golden hills

California gold! The history of the settlement of California is tied to the lust for gold—the mineral kind. However, those who came with the strike-it-rich fever but eventually turned to farming unknowingly brought with them another kind of gold—renewable gold—that we see today on the hills surrounding San Francisco Bay. These hills turn a tawny golden color after the rains stop, usually in May. The gold of the ripening wild rye and wild oats that escaped from early grain farms is sustained by the nitrogen that settles on the hills as a byproduct of the internal combustion engine. Purple needlegrass, California's best known native grass, was able to grow on soils lacking in nitrogen and gave the hills a green color. Today's golden hills are accented by the dark green of the coastal oaks that grow in the ravines and on the slopes of the hills. These two contrasting colors make endlessly beautiful patterns along the roads of the Bay Area throughout the summer. The turkey vultures that soar along the rims of these golden hills are carried aloft on updrafts created by the rising heat of the long days. The heat and their effortless flight combine into a feeling of a California summer.
pjm

driving golden hills
his deafness doesn't matter—
there's no need to speak
        pjm

my soldier grandson
home for his twenty-first birthday—
golden summer hills
        Carol Steele

Photos: Ed Grossmith (Dudleya, previous page), Garry Gay

summer fog

This fog can also be called coastal or ocean fog. During much of the summer, a great fog bank hangs over the central California coast and many neighborhoods of San Francisco. The fog is caused by cooling of moisture-laden winds from the Pacific Ocean when they pass over a cold current of coastal waters. The fog extends inland until it reaches sun-warmed slopes or lowlands, where it evaporates without a trace.

     The varying cloud cover leads to great contrasts in weather between the coast and inland valleys. Unwary travelers are likely to become chilled when they dress for sunny inland skies and encounter the cold, windy, foggy coast. This season word can imply the possibility of a significant change of circumstances.
pg

summer fog
somewhere the beach
somewhere me
                Roger Abe

Point Reyes
ocean fog curls up over
the cliff between us
                Yvonne Hardenbrook

summer fog
young women gossiping
about boy friends
                Jerry Ball

Photo: Garry Gay

wildland fire

July, August and September are the months when firefighters in California worry most about wildland fires. Rains usually end in May and often do not return until mid-October. In late summer and early autumn, hillside grasses and resinous chaparral shrubs are completely dry, and any little spark can start a conflagration—a lightning strike, a carelessly thrown match or cigarette butt, a rancher's tractor hitting a rock, a spark from a passing train, fireworks.

    When a wildfire starts, the firefighter's first responsibility is to save lives and homes. Most rural areas are protected by volunteers. The pager goes off, and the firefighter dashes for uniform, boots and firepack as adrenalin takes over. A quick drive to the firehouse, and soon the siren is wailing from the truck. The hot fire adds to the hot weather, and the firefighter sweats heavily under the yellow fireproof uniform and struggles to breathe through the smoke. If the fire reaches a forest, the California Division of Forestry is called in and takes charge. If the fire is a large one, more companies are called in along with helicopters with water buckets and cargoes of fire retardant. When the wildfire has been put out, many concerns remain, even if human lives and homes have not been lost. What has happened to livestock and grain? wild animals and plants? When the rains come later in the year, the bare, burned-over land will be susceptible to mud slides.
amh

wildfire
the thermometer climbs
all night
               Carolyn Hall
                First place, SF International Haiku Contest (2000)
                Mariposa #4 (2001)
                Water Lines, John Barlow, ed. Snapshot Press, UK (2006)

Photo: Anne M. Homan

HUMAN AFFAIRS

Bay to Breakers Race

Since 1911, the Bay to Breakers Race has taken place in San Francisco on the third Sunday in May. Participants run twelve kilometers from the Embarcadero to the Pacific Ocean. This race has become the most important running event of the year in the Bay Area. Up to 100,000 serious and not-so-serious contestants jam the streets of San Francisco for a running street party. Outrageous costumes, such as a thirteen-foot tall carrot and a woman with a water faucet on her head, are traditional. The race is imbued with a sort of Mardi gras spirit of fun.
amh

Bay to Breakers
running alone with the shade
of my partner
                  Anne M. Homan

Bay to Breakers—
the long fluid strides
of brothers
                  Carolyn Thomas

even the serious
runner caught laughing
Bay to Breakers Race
                  Anne M. Homan

Bay to Breakers Race
some runners tilt to the right
some to the left
                  Zinovy Vayman

Photo: John Lankes

ANIMALS

anise swallowtail
Papilio zelicaon

The *Papilionidae* family of butterflies, called the swallowtails, is distinguished by the tail that extends from the back of the lower wings. They are large butterflies. The anise swallowtail is yellow with black on the wing edges and in toward the body, which is also black. It frequents the Pacific Coast and the high plains of the west. Its pale green eggs are smooth and spherical. The young caterpillars are black with orange spots; later they become green with black bands. If disturbed, like all swallowtail caterpillars, they will suddenly evert bright orange "stinkhorns" that give off a foul odor from just behind their heads. The eggs are laid on parsley-like plants in the carrot family like fennel and anise. Its favorite flowers for feeding are lantana, fennel, anise, zinnia, butterfly bush and lily-of-the-nile. It has been observed "hilltopping" on Mt. Hamilton. (See "hilltopping" in spring section.)
pjm

boulevard traffic—
the anise swallowtail's
enduring ballet
                pjm

Watercolor: Lisa Hill

gopher snake
Pituophis melanoleucus catenifer

All snakes are cold-blooded, and the Pacific gopher snake, like all snakes, is mostly visible in the Bay Area summer when the weather is warm. On small, local roads, they like especially to stretch out on the macadam in late afternoon. The snake is yellow to cream-colored with black or brown dorsal splotches, usually more widely spaced on the tail than on the body. The *caternifer* subspecies has gray dots on the sides of its body and underneath its tail. The dorsal scales are keeled. A large snake, adult specimens have been measured from 36 to 110 inches. In the Bay Area it is common in grassland and open brushland. When disturbed by humans, the gopher snake often hisses loudly, flattens its head and vibrates its tail. Because of this behavior, it is sometimes mistaken for a rattlesnake and killed. The snake preys upon rodents, rabbits, birds and occasionally lizards, killing them by constriction. From June through August, the gopher snake lays from one to two clutches of eggs. It is a good climber and burrower.
amh

at the front doorstep
coils stiff in early morning
a small gopher snake
                Anne M. Homan

gopher snake
the previously unknown
friends show up
                Alison Woolpert

Photo: Scott Hein (www.heinphoto.com)

midshipman
Porichthys notatus

The northern midshipman, also called singing fish, bullhead or toadfish, is a member of the toadfish family. It is distinguished by its extended and protruding eyes and numerous rows of photophores (small, shiny button-like lenses) on the head and along the body and the small first dorsal fin. Perhaps the photophores reminded the species' discoverer of the buttons on the uniform of an old-time midshipman. The fish has a broad head, large mouth and lower projecting jaw. Its color is dark blue to grayish brown, fading to lighter sides and a yellowish belly; its size can range up to 15 inches. From Mexico to Alaska, it spawns in the spring in shallow waters along the Pacific Coast. It is recorded as an edible species but is favored locally as bait for shark fishing.

    In the 1980's a mysterious phenomenon around San Francisco Bay waters came to public attention. Local residents reported a strange humming sound that could not be identified, coming from the bay. Speculations about the source of the sound ran rife from UFOs to secret naval experiments. Research proved it to be the singing of the male midshipman (in the photo the large fish in the middle), who produces the sound to attract females (in the photo the female is to the right of the male, a cluster of baby midshipmen to his left) to the nest he has built. Local people living on the water in boats or houseboats say the noise is like a loud refrigerator and is detrimental to sleep and rest.
ra

drinks on the terrace
of his bachelor's pad—
the midshipman's song
                Linda Papanicolaou

Photo: Margaret Marchaterre

smelt
Hyomesus pretiosus

    The surf smelt, *Hyomesus pretiosus*, sometimes known as silver smelt, day-fish or perlin, is pale green with a silver belly and a pronounced metallic stripe along the sides that turns dark when the fish is removed from the water. The maximum size is about 10 inches. The male becomes brown on the back at spawning time in the summer. The surf smelt occurs from Pt. Conception to Alaska. While declined in numbers from the past, smelt remain an important forage fish. They are taken mostly by hook and throw nets.
    The night smelt, *Spirinchus starski*, also known as whitebait, sand smelt or nightfish, is a very pale green fish with a silvery stripe on the side, with a maximum size of 10 inches. It belongs to the family of long-finned smelt. Its range is from Pismo Beach to the Juan de Fuca Strait. These smelt are mostly taken by dip or A-frame nets.
    As the names indicate, some species enter the very shallow surf zones for spawning during the daytime and others at night. The fish prefer certain conditions for spawning: tides, moon phase, surf conditions and sand type all come into play. Experienced fishermen can tell exactly the type/quality of wave that the fish will come in on. In the daytime, with clear water, the fish can be seen streaking into the surf. At night, nets are dipped blindly. Net dippers are sometimes surprised—finding in their nets from nothing to several gallons of smelt to a predatory fish that had been following the smelt. The A-frame dip net design is based on nets used for millennia by indigenous peoples.
ra

roar of the surf
silvery scales glistening
on the netted smelt
              Anne M. Homan

smelt run
young men scanning the surf
at high tide
              Jerry Ball

water turtles

When the summer sun beams down on ponds and rivers, the water turtles make their presence most fully known. With enviable leisure and clumsy grace, they scrabble onto logs, stones and banks to bask in the warmth. Sometimes they pile up on one another, turtle on turtle, and with astonishing acrobatic skill manage to balance on a bobbing log. The sun draws them out as it does a thermometer's mercury. One can do a turtle count on a familiar log and arrive at a subjective determination of the degree of heat. And, if they happen to tumble off their perch, taking a few others along into the cooling water, they make their way unperturbed back to a sunny spot. Often we are rewarded with only a quick splash as one, then another, slips into the safety of the water if we happen to step too close. Sunning turtles—a sure sign of high summer.

  The most common water turtle in the San Francisco Bay Area is the western pond turtle, *Clemmys marmorata*. It varies from about 3 ½ to 7 ½ inches in length. It is dark brown or black, usually with yellowish or brown markings on the carapace. A clutch of 3-11 eggs is laid between April and August, depending on the weather. Plants, insects, carrion, worms and fish make up the water turtle's diet.

es

reflecting pool . . .
claw marks of a turtle
on the submerged stone
    Ebba Story

sultry afternoon
turtle noses stipple
the glossy lake
    Ebba Story

turtle island
we slide off the beach . . .
only our noses show
    Roger Abe

Photo: Patrick Gallagher

PLANTS

beach primrose
Camissonia cheiranthifolia

A small plant with small yellow flowers, a member of the suncup family, the beach primrose grows flat to the ground on sandy dunes, with its arms radiating out from the center. Sometimes it forms large, spreading mats of gray-green sparsely dotted with simple, yellow, four-petaled flowers. It is this simplicity, this uncomplicatedness that we find appealing.
pjm

where the beach primrose
wanders a sign says "Caution"
in very small print
              pjm

Photo: Neil Kramer (Kramer Botanical)

beach sagewort
Artemesia pycnocephala

Beach sagewort grows along sandy beaches of bays and oceans. It has a fern-like form with stems that grow form a central plant upward in graceful fronds that change over the seasons. It has an independent stance—a come-what-may-I'll-still-be-here-look. In the spring its new gray-green leaves are delicate and lacy and its young pliable stems bounce with ease in the spring wind. As the year progresses into summer, barely noticeable yellow flowers, like small nubs, fill out the ends of the lacy fronds and give them a yellowish cast. The stems have become thicker now, more woody, necessary to hold the fuller frond heads.
pjm

heads of beach sagewort
nodding to each other like
ladies gossiping
        Kiyoko Tokutomi

in the shape
of the Pacific wind
weathered sagewort
        Karina Young

beach sagewort
mirrors a sunless sky
quietly ... quiet
        Judith Schallberger

seeded sagewort
we discuss the diagnosis
behind closed doors
        Alison Woolpert

graceful sand dunes
silver-green *Artemesia*
a vast *corps de ballet*
        Joan Zimmerman

Photo: Ed Grossmith

coyote mint
Monardella odoratissima

If we brush against the leafy stems, we will appreciate the strong mint aroma. We might even smell it before rounding a switchback. Rub it and our fingers trail mint scent down the path. This tall perennial (½ to 1½ feet) has purplish-pink blossoms that are a delightful find in the coastal scrub or open rocky terrain. The prominent lance-like leaves have veins that seem to be impressed on the upper side and ridged below. There is a fringe of hairs at the top of each tiny calyx tube that makes up the "flower" head.
dcg

switchback
smiling at coyote mint
before I see it
        D. Claire Gallagher

Photo: © Br. Alfred Brousseau, Saint Mary's College

elderberry
Sambucus mexicana

Summer begins gently with elderberry blossoms. The flat-topped white clusters are neither lush nor flashy, but an important sign of summer. This often treelike large shrub with its toothed oval leaflets is common along streams, meadows and country lanes. By late summer or early autumn, the blossoms become clusters of deep blue berries, used by early settlers to make jelly, pie filling and wine. The white stem pith can be easily removed, and the Indians used the hollow tubes to make whistles and to blow coals alive for a fire. Some California Indians called the elderberry the "tree of music." However, the stems must be thoroughly dry before placing them in the mouth because the roots, stems and leaves are toxic. Indians in the Bay Area used elderberry blossoms as an environmental indicator that shellfish were no longer a safe food. By the time the berries were ripe, shellfish were again safe to eat.
dcg

returning
to the old homestead—
elderberry blossoms
    Carolyn Thomas

trail marker
the bicycle tracks end
at the elderberry
    Cindy Tebo

the smooth hollow
of this bedrock mortar
elderberry flowers
    D. Claire Gallagher

the rocking chair creaks
with the rhythm of his tale
elderberry pie
    Anne M. Homan

Photo: Keir Morse

evening primrose
Oenothera hookeri

The evening primrose has large, bright yellow flowers that open in early evening from June through September. It is an erect plant from two to four feet high with a thick stalk. The oval-tipped leaves are four to nine inches long. Stem, leaves and buds are covered with soft white hairs. The plant is most often found in coastal areas, not on beaches, but in moist lowlands. It is easily grown from seed. The showy flower has four yellow petals. The individual blooms are short lived, yet the plant continues to flower for months. In mid-summer the lower stems have maturing seed capsules while buds are still developing and opening at the top of the stalk.
dc

my son and I
discuss the living will—
evening primrose
        Linda Papanicolaou

she toys
with the edge of his kerchief
evening primrose
        Ebba Story

fading light
I close my book to peruse
an evening primrose
        Ebba Story

Photo: Jo-Ann Ordano @ California Academy of Sciences

farewell-to-spring
Clarkia, spp.

When we see the profusion of farewell-to-spring blossoms, we know what perhaps we have already felt: spring has given way to summer. The four-petaled cups open too late to hold the last of the California seasonal rains. Instead the blossoms splash the grasses in the drying hillsides with hues of rose, lavender and purple. A genus of great variety, each petal of the best-known species, *Clarkia amoena*, is at least 1½ inches long. The plants themselves vary from wind-stunted along the dunes to two-foot tall inland. The showy blooms grow closely along the stem and furl their petals at night, almost as if retreating a little from evening chill. Their early June blooms herald the beginning of summer.
dcg

by a flower
called farewell-to-spring
my grown daughter
              Paul O. Williams

Photo: Scott Peden

hens-and-chickens, live-forever
Dudleya farinosa

The live-forever is a coastal succulent of the stonecrop family. Its oval leaves grow in a rosette, with the rosettes growing in clusters that emanate outward from the central "hen." Each rosette sends up a long red stem from its side in summer, atop which bloom pale yellow flowers. The one to two inch basal leaves often have a grayish cast with a mealy substance that will rub off. Another of its common names is powdery dudleya. The plant is found clinging to coastal cliffs in Oregon and California.
pjm

dudleya
in headland pockets—
little hands in Nana's
          D. Claire Gallagher

bright live-forever
on the golden shore
boys digging sand palaces
          Joan Zimmerman

Grandma's garden
hens and chickens
spreading out
          Jerry Ball

I strain to hear
the live-forevers' chatter
above the beach waves
          donnalynn chase

flora of the dunes
   will the winner please stand up
      it's Dudleya!
          Ed Grossmith

Photo: Ed Grossmith

mantilija poppy
Romneya coulteri

The mantilija poppy is a stately perennial shrub, growing four to eight foot tall. Its gray/blue-green leaves are deeply cut. From May to July the startling flowers that resemble fried eggs appear, but they can even be found until the first hard frost. They can grow up to nine inches wide with five to six petals that look like crepe paper. In the middle of the petals is a mass of golden-yellow fragrant stamens. Individual plants and occasional patches of them occur in dry washes, canyons and with coastal sage. They range from the Santa Cruz Mountains south to San Diego County. They are prolific along portions of Los Gatos Creek, which flows into the south end of San Francisco Bay.
dc

mindfulness
demanded by a patch of
mantilija poppies
        donnalynn chase

mantilija poppy
one bloom hogging the middle
of the driveway
        Alison Woolpert

Photo: Rebecca Davies

mariposa tulip
Calochortus luteus and *Calochortus venustus*

The mariposa tulip features flowers with spotted markings that cause the petals to resemble butterfly wings—hence, the name "mariposa," the Spanish word for butterfly. Luteus is yellow with bright yellow petals and spots, sometimes with dark brown lines. The white petals of Venustus are often flushed with pink or purple and marked with a variety of splotches. They are both found extensively in the San Francisco Bay area, blooming in open places in the drier foothills and mountains from the very end of spring through summer when the hillside grasses have dried. They vary from about six inches to one foot in height. The long narrow leaves are lance-shaped with the parallel veins typical of the lily family.

pg

Photo: Patrick Gallagher

sand verbena
Abronia latifolia
and *Abronia umbellata*

The sand verbena is a creeper on sandy beaches and dunes that dies back in winter and extends itself in voluptuous abundance in the summer. The flowers grow in heads like small umbrellas. *Latifolia*, the yellow verbena, has a more succulent leaf than the pink beach verbena, *umbellata*. The leaves are shaped like tiny lily pads.
pjm

yellow verbena
poking through the boardwalk
get-away weekend
              D. Claire Gallagher

Photo: Anne Homan

soap plant
Chlorogalum pomeridianum

Named for the use of its bulb, which when crushed and mixed with water produces a sudsy solution, the soap plant has many other uses well known to Native Americans. With the skin of the bulb, they extracted fibers that they made into brushes; the bulb itself was crushed and spread on ponds or a slow stream to stupefy fish. They also baked the bulb and ate it; this food was called amole.

The plant is abundant in many areas of California. Its winter appearance is like that of a coarse rosette of grass having blue-green leaves with wavy edges. A narrow green stalk appears in the spring and branches as it grows higher. Many delicate spidery five-petaled white flowers bloom in the summer, but only open late in the day.
dcg

picking soaproot flowers at sunset
my hands
fill with stars
                Laurie Stoelting

Photo: Beatrice F. Howitt © California Academy of Sciences

tarweed
Madia spp.

In the summer after most other wild flowers have gone to seed, tarweed and its relatives come into their own. Spread out over grasslands or along roadsides in colorful masses up to three feet high, the California native survives hot dry weather with several defenses. It has an odor somewhat like kerosene, which makes it unappetizing for grazing animals, and it has a sticky substance covering its stem and leaves, which keeps moisture in the plant from evaporating in the heat. Elegant tarweed has small yellow daisy-like flowers with deep crimson centers. The flowers open in the late afternoon, stay open all night and close in the worst heat of midday.
amh

resiny tarweed
pungent still on my fingers
why did I pick it?
                      Anne M. Homan
                First Dream, Two Autumns, 1998

Photo: Barbara Mallon

yellow star thistle
Centaura solstitialis

Like many residents of the state, yellow star thistle is not a native Californian. It came from the Mediterranean area, and scientists have found its seeds here in 19th-century adobe bricks. By 1997, the rapidly spreading pest had spread to over 20 million acres of California grassland. The thistle leafs up after wild oats and native wildflowers, blooming in the summer dry season. Eventually, it chokes out native plants and grasses. Although cattle can eat the plant, it is not as nutritious as grass. Horses that eat too much of it can die. Researchers are trying to find natural enemies of the plant to import here; they are also working on an effective herbicide.

      The bright yellow, fluffy-looking flowerhead is surrounded by long spines that can deliver a very painful wound. The stems and leaves, however, are not spiny.
amh

straying from the path
my daydreams are stabbed
by a star thistle
                Anne M. Homan

Photo: Dick Finn

AUTUMN

SKY AND ELEMENTS

first rain

The first rain, after summer's prolonged heat and drought, is eagerly awaited in the San Francisco Bay Area. Its arrival is normally about mid-October. The first rain has a special aroma, perhaps because we have not smelled it in so long. Often, by the time it arrives, we have become anxious, wondering if this will be a year when drought will wreak its havoc on nature and agriculture. We are impatient for the hot days to be over. We yearn for green hills and clear skies free of dust and smog. The first rain can be a traffic hazard because it makes oil-slick roads slippery. Usually this rain comes on a gray, cloudy day rather than with the white cumulus of a thunderstorm.
amh

fingers in rhythm
knitting by the window
first rain
        Elaine and Neal Whitman

Photo: Patrick Gallagher ("Migrating Butterflies," previous page), Michael Pocha

LANDSCAPE

brown hills

Green hills, gold hills, brown hills. The sensuous hills of the Bay Area landscape change color with the seasons. In the wet season, they become an intense green, perhaps compensating for their dry season makeover. As winter and spring rains end, hill grasses gradually turn the ripe gold of harvest. Green-leafed oaks in the arroyos make a sharp contrast. By late summer, however, without a scythe or tractor to cut down nature's largesse, the grasses become a duller shade. In areas where the hills are used for grazing, the golden seed heads disappear. The dust of summer's drought takes its toll; large cracks appear in clay soils. Wildflower and grass seeds hitchhike on unsuspecting passersby. Brown hills now bear the sun's heat until the cycle continues with the first rains. Occasionally, a year will come when the wet season does not arrive. Then the hills become an even deeper brown as the remaining grasses are stamped into the soil by wildlife and livestock. The cracks become wider and deeper.
amh

tawny hills—
a sign advises
keep your children near
                Linda Papanicolaou

Photo: Don Homan

HUMAN AFFAIRS

San Francisco Military Fleet Week

Even though the Navy presence has left San Francisco, the city continues to celebrate Fleet Week every year on the second week in October. Typically, to begin the week's festivities, about a dozen ships, outlined by streams of water from circling fireboats, pass under the Golden Gate Bridge on Saturday morning, their crews crisply lined up at attention along the decks. Thousands of spectators watch from shore; others on sailboats bob on the waves. The Blue Angels perform their aerial acrobatics overhead. In 1999 the warship parade included the aircraft carrier *USS Abraham Lincoln*, two nuclear subs, an attack ship, a destroyer, a cruiser and a frigate among others. The lead ship, attack ship *USS Essex*, fired a 19-gun salute as it came into the harbor. After the parade, many of the ships are open to public tours at San Francisco, Oakland and Alameda docks.
amh

screaming Blue Angels
high above our flapping sails
Fleet Week on the bay
                Anne M. Homan

Photos: Don Homan

ANIMALS

acorn woodpecker
Melanerpes formicivorus

In the autumn months acorn woodpeckers work together in small, noisy community groups to store acorns into dead trees. One huge valley oak skeleton can be lined with hundreds of acorns stuffed into previously drilled holes; the same woodpeckers use this in one season. Their call of *ja-cob, ja-cob* can be heard in oak woods and mixed oak/pine forests. Besides acorns and nuts in the autumn, acorn woodpeckers eat insects, tree sap and fruit. The acorn woodpecker is easily identifiable by its black back and clownish black, white and red head. About 8 to 9½ inches, in flight the bird has a large, white rump and white wing patches. Its nest is inside a hole in a tree or pole.

The red topknot feathers were used by California Native Americans as basket decoration. Since the feathers are only about 3/8 inch in length, the weaver used special techniques to incorporate them in her basket. One Pomo gift basket woven in the year 1900 contains topknot feathers from 200 acorn woodpeckers. As California's environment has become more and more choked with asphalt and houses, this woodpecker is much rarer than it used to be. Preserving dead snags in parks and wilderness areas is very important to the bird's continued survival.
amh

drawn out bear market . . .
acorn woodpeckers stuffing
their oak granary
    Anne M. Homan

Photos: Patrick Gallagher

California quail
allipepla californica

Drivers often see grown quail scurrying across a country road in autumn or winter, when they're more gregarious and live in coveys. The California quail is a plump bird about 10 inches tall with a plumage of many colors; its genus name, *Callipepla*, means "beautiful coat." Shades of gray, brown and white blend together in patterns on their backs and bellies. The male has a black bib with a white border and a white headband. Both male and female have a short black plume curling forward from the crown; the female's is somewhat smaller. The normal call is three-toned, variously rendered as *Chi-ca´-go* or *Where are´ you*? Their nest is formed in a grass-lined hollow in the ground; the female lays from 10 to 17 eggs. Sometimes they have two broods in a season. They search out seeds and insects on the ground and roost in trees at night.

    For the last four years, we have had quail nesting under bushes at the side of our house. The male often struts along our deck on his delicate feet and insistently stakes his territorial claim, *kurr*. Later, when the chicks have hatched and are mobile, the male and female take turns watching over their brood. One stands up on the deck or on a similar high place while the other stays on the ground with the chicks, hunting for food.
amh

covey of quail
dusting themselves . . .
soft twilight shadows
          Anne M. Homan

whispered secrets
the bobble
of a quail's topknot
          Carolyn Hall
          Water Lines, John Barlow, ed.
          Snapshot Press, UK (2006)

evening stillness
the shift
of a quail's head
          Carolyn Thomas

paying bills—
out the window
quail at the feeder
          Laurabell

Artist: Floy Zittin

migrating monarchs
Danaus plexippus

Early American colonists named this butterfly after the Prince of Orange. Its black-veined orange wings are dramatic and very recognizable. Each autumn the entire surviving populations of monarch butterflies born west of the Rockies in the U.S. and Canada migrate south to California. Hundreds of thousands of these monarchs congregate to winter in Bay Area habitats. Beginning in mid-October, sightseers watch monarchs gathering in protected groves in Santa Cruz, Pacific Grove and Fremont, and other groves farther south. Hundreds of monarchs lazily wing about each grove on warm, sunny days. On cool or overcast days, observers see only large clumps of "dried leaves" until some of the dull brown "leaves" flutter or open for a moment to a flash of orange. It may take a while to discern tens of thousands of monarch butterflies huddling together for warmth and safety, enveloping the branches of a few trees. Although monarchs return to the same groves every year, they do not necessarily return to the same trees; in fact, in one season they may shift to different trees.

    These monarchs in the Bay Area roam to find nectar near the over-wintering sites if the weather becomes warm. In late February or early March, or earlier if the winter is mild, they mate before gradually departing northward. Along the way north, the monarchs find milkweed and lay their eggs. It is the butterflies that result from metamorphosis of the caterpillars from these eggs who continue to the summering grounds. Over the summer the metamorphosis is repeated continuously. In most cases it is the great-grandchildren of the over-wintering individuals who arrive at the winter havens the following year. Monarch larvae feed on milkweed which is toxic; however, the butterflies are chemically protected from the poisonous sap. The poison residue in the adults makes them distasteful to most predators

    Monarchs from east of the Rockies wing down to Mexico each fall. Celebrants of *El Dia de los Muertos* (the Day of the Dead) scan the sky for returning butterflies—symbols of returning souls of departed loved ones.

dcg

pinned to the gray sky
a monarch butterfly
struggles in the wind
          Roger Abe

winter monarchs
the flutter of
tour bus ladies
          D. Claire Gallagher

closed curtains signal
that she has already gone—
migrating monarchs
          Carol Steele

copper sunset
the stillness
of wintering butterflies
          Carolyne Rohrig

Photo: Anne M. Homan

migrating raptors

Beginning roughly August 20 and continuing until about December 20, tens of thousands of hawks, eagles, falcons and vultures migrate southward over the Golden Gate from their breeding grounds to their wintering grounds. Over 19 species, including the osprey, white-tailed kite, northern harrier, red-tailed hawk, red-shouldered hawk, golden eagle and Cooper's hawk, make the journey. Hawk Hill, in the Marin headlands just northwest of the Golden Gate Bridge, is one of the best viewing sites. The nearby Marin Headlands Visitor Center has an excellent presentation about the migration. The Golden Gate Raptor Observatory studies this autumn migration with a few professionals and more than 250 volunteers.
amh

Photo: Ed Grossmith

purple-striped jelly
Chrysaora colorata

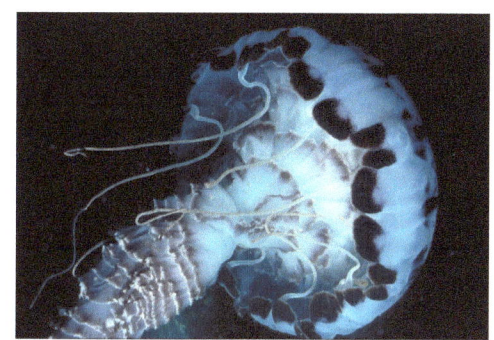

Purple-striped jellyfish live along the California coast. In the strong tides and storms of autumn, they are often torn apart on the shoreline rocks. Colorful shreds of them appear on the beach after a storm. Unlike some jellies, they do not live in large aggregations. The bell of this jelly, streaked with a pattern of stripes, can attain diameters of 27 inches. Four white frilly tentacles flow from its mouth, and eight narrow purple tentacles dangle from the margins of its bell. All of the tentacles can deliver a painful sting. Young jellies can have tentacles as long as 4 to 5 meters flowing out behind them. Zooplankton such as copepods, larval fish and fish eggs serve as prey. Tiny juvenile slender crabs often hitch rides on the purple-striped jelly's mouth tentacles and scavenge some of the jelly's food until they let go and drift down to start their adult life at the ocean's bottom.
amh

the thickness
of the glass between us—
purple-striped jelly
        Linda Papanicolaou

purple-striped jelly—
flotilla of pelicans
backpedaling!
        pjm
        Blush of Winter Moon

Translucent surf
sunlight through
the purple-striped jelly
        Garry Gay

Photo: Lovell and Libby Langstroth

tarantula
Eurypelma californicum

Except during mating season this reclusive spider, often called the hairy tarantula, emerges only at night; it feeds within a radius of a few feet from its burrow and is rarely seen. A giant, it is four inches long when the legs are extended and is covered with long, dark brown hairs with barbs at the ends. When disturbed, it may rub hind legs on the top of the hairy abdomen to loosen these hairs and fling them at aggressors. These hairs irritate the skin and mucous membranes of their predators. Although ferocious in appearance, this tarantula is not aggressive. When it does bite, its venom is no more toxic than a bee's sting.

Hairy tarantula males leave their seclusion to search for mates in the foothills on early evenings in late August and September. They lumber across fields and clearings. After mating, a male attempts a hasty goodbye before the female can kill him. In any case the male is soon to die. After ten years to grow to maturity, his life span ends after mating. The larger female may live for 25 years, raising many broods of young. A sac of eggs are laid several weeks after mating and guarded in the female's burrow. Hatchlings disperse about six weeks later.

The name tarantula derives from Taranto, Italy where the townspeople engaged in a frenzied dance during the Middle Ages. They claimed the dancing was the remedy for the bite of a local spider. The music became known as the Tarantella, and the spider the tarantula. New World tarantulas are actually not related to the Old World "wolf spider."

Another species of tarantula lives in the California foothills. This "smooth" tarantula is velvety, half the size of the hairy tarantula, and much more pugnacious.
dcg

abracadabra—
the hairy tarantula
waves his arms at me
        pjm

Photo: Matt Knoth

PLANTS

bigleaf maple
Acer macrophyllum

As noted in its scientific and common name, the lobed leaves of this maple are very large. The tree inhabits riparian corridors in the Bay Area, where it is most noticeable in the autumn for its vivid yellow-orange foliage. In the spring it has long, drooping clusters of fragrant yellowish flowers, four to six inches long, which are followed by the development of the paired winged "keys," or samara. The tree can grow to 100 feet, and when the crown is free of nearby trees, it will spread out.

      The wood is used for furniture, paneling and veneer. Native Americans made paddles of it. The seeds are enjoyed by squirrels, chipmunks and some songbirds. The sap is supposedly of a good quality for making maple syrup.
amh

bigleaf maple—
the sculptor strokes his thumb
across the burl
                Linda Papanicolaou

Photo: Phyllis Lasche

buckeye
Aesculus californica

As the round, leathery fruit pod of this tree dries, it reveals the satiny gold-brown nut, called a buckeye. The name comes from the fact that as the drying fruit pod splits open, the emergent nut, or buckeye, looks like an eye within eyelids, perhaps like the brown eye of a deer. Buckeyes are roughly spherical, about two to three inches in diameter. In early fall after the leaves are gone, the fruits bob from the branches in the wind before they eventually drop to the ground.

    The California buckeye tree has adapted a unique method to deal with the state's long hot, dry season. In late summer or early autumn, long before any other deciduous trees have lost their leaves, the buckeye's leaves will shrivel and turn brown. The large leaves are opposite and palmately compound. Leaves, nuts, and young twigs can be poisonous to livestock. Native Americans threw ground-up nuts in streams to stun fish in order to capture them for food. Although buckeyes are poisonous, in years of poor acorn harvest when hunger loomed, Native Americans gathered them and carefully detoxified them by leaching.

    Buckeye trees grow in the foothills of the Bay Area. In early summer they are easily distinguished from neighboring oaks by their candle-shaped white flower clusters. The flowers have a delicate fragrance and are attractive to many native butterflies. Some beekeepers accuse buckeye nectar of being poisonous to bees.

amh

plump buckeye fruit
tugging down the bare branch-end—
midlife pregnancy
                Joan Zimmerman
                Frogpond 2010

Photo: Rebecca Davies

buckwheat
Eriogonium latifolium

One of the distinctive autumn sights among the browns and greens of the coastal dunes is the buckwheat. Its white pompon blossoms are profuse and long-lasting, covering the woody branches of the plant. The flowers begin in August and often continue blooming into November. Young flowers are white with a tinge of purple. As they mature, they become whiter until they go to seed. Even then, they are distinctive in that the seeds retain the pompon shape as they dry, turning a noticeable rusty brown. The plant grows to about one to two feet tall. The leaves are in a cluster at the bottom of the stem. The leaf blades are wavy and oblong with a white wooly surface underneath.
pjm/dcg

the setting sun
creeps through the stalks of buckwheat
dyeing them
        Buson (trans. by R.H. Blythe)

Buckwheat
gone to seed
your hidden love letters
        Garry Gay

Photo: Susan Williams

clematis
Clematis lasiantha

The wild clematis is a trailing vine that blooms from March to June in the Bay Area chaparral, climbing over any available shrub or plant for support. In autumn, the plant is sometimes called "old man's beard" because the female flowers have developed into striking white plumes for the winds to pull apart and scatter. The spring flower has four cream-colored petals with a center of many cream-colored stamens or several greenish-yellow pistils, according to its sex. The plant's compound leaves are in groups of three, five or seven, but most often in three, making it similar to poison oak, over which it sometimes grows.

The cultivated clematis, developed from the wild species, is a familiar showy vine in Bay Area gardens.
amh

Photo: © Br. Alfred Brousseau, Saint Mary's College

huckleberry
Vaccinium ovatum

Plump blue-black berries ripen on this shrub from September to November. It is often the dominant plant in the under-story in coastal Douglas fir and redwood forests. Bushes closer to the coast grow taller than those in the Oakland hills; they can reach eight feet high. The small horizontal toothed evergreen leaves are shiny and stand out in the winter woods. Pink bell-shaped flowers, similar to the manzanita, bloom in April and May. The delicious sweet berries can be substituted in any recipe calling for blueberries. Sometimes the berries are covered with a whitish bloom—this is a naturally occurring yeast that is edible and actually makes the berries even sweeter to the taste. These berries were favorites with the grizzlies, the only native bears who lived in the Bay Area.
pg

Portola Park
around the settler's cabin
sweet huckleberries
            Patrick Gallagher

empty baskets
he admits he has forgotten
where the huckleberries are
            Cindy Tebo

Photo: Patrick Gallagher

oak apple, oak gall

In the autumn white oak trees seem to bear a crop of apples. The buff-colored balls are in fact inedible insect galls, tumors created by the tree in reaction to the irritation of eggs inserted in the tree's branches by a species of gallfly, a tiny black wasp. The gall serves as both shelter and food for the gallfly larvae when they hatch from the eggs. By late fall the galls have turned brown and the adult gallflies have escaped through a pin-prick sized hole. Galls are most noticeable in the fall and winter seasons when the deciduous oaks are bare of leaves. Oak galls have been used commercially for tanning and dying because of their high tannic acid content.
dcg

oak gall's lightness
of weathered, brittle skin
and fleshy nursery
                Anne M. Homan

Photo: Anne M. Homan

pickleweed
Salicornia virginica

Pickleweed, a homely succulent, stands out in the autumn with its orange-red color. The plant thrives in the tidal salt water of San Francisco Bay Area marshes, but unfortunately, many of these marshes have been filled in, so the habitat of the pickleweed has been severely affected. Since 1850, some 194,000 acres of salt marsh around the bay have declined to about 30,000. Two endangered species, the salt marsh harvest mouse and the clapper rail, are dependent on this plant for shelter and nesting areas. Many other shorebirds use the plant's tangled 18-inch high thickets for shelter and roosting as well. "Glasswort," another name for the plant, derives from the burning of the plant to supply soda ash for glassmaking. "Sea asparagus" and "poor man's asparagus" are other names for the pickleweed because people harvest its tender tips, which can be eaten fresh, steamed or pickled. Pickleweed appears to be leafless and flowerless, but its minute leaves and flowers are hidden in the joints of the cylindrical stems. The greenish flowers, which have no petals, bloom from July through November.
amh

Elkhorn Slough maze
branching through the pickleweed
the lost kayakers
        Joan Zimmerman

Photo: Courtesy of the Elkhorn Slough Foundation

rattlesnake grass
Briza maxima

By autumn rattlesnake grass flower spikelets have turned to gold and hang in drooping panicles that shake in the wind. These spikelets are inflated and resemble the rattles on the end of a rattlesnake's tail. The plant's leaves are typically grass-like, with a few along the stem and the rest in a compact clump at the base. Rattlesnake grass is an annual and stands about 12 to 18 inches tall. A native of Europe, it has managed to escape from California gardens where it is sometimes cultivated as an ornamental. We often see patches of them growing at Asilomar.
amh

even without him
I didn't sleep very well—
dry rattlesnake grass
           donnalynn chase

Photo: © Br. Alfred Brousseau, Saint Mary's College

snowberry
Symphoricarpos albus laevigatus

In the autumn season the snowberry develops the small clusters of white spongy berries for which it is named. Although not poisonous, the berries have an insipid, sometimes soapy, taste to humans, but birds enjoy them. The plant is a shrub, from one to six feet tall, growing in small colonies in Bay Area woodlands. Its leaves are paired along the stem. Some of the leaves are a simple, oval shape, while others have small scallops or lobes in no consistent pattern. The tiny pink, bell-shaped flowers appear from May to July.
amh

Photo: Beatrice F. Howitt © California Academy of Sciences

ticking leaves

You are at the edge of a woodland, on a park bench near a sycamore, or under a meadow tree on an Indian summer day. Perhaps your back is against a maple; perhaps you are on a hill with a view; perhaps you are accompanied by a companion comfortable with silence.

    Listen well, beyond the obvious sounds. You may hear a sound like insects clicking. The sun's warmth is drying fallen leaves. As they contract, their desiccating tissue ticks or clicks—a subtle sound, a small snapping. Once you hear it, you can hear ticking from drying leaves all around you if you stop to listen.
dcg

from every direction
the click of drying leaves—
your one-way ticket
                D. Claire Gallagher

Photo: June Hopper Hymas

western hopbush
Ptelea crenulata

The hopbush stands out in the fall and late summer because of its dangling fruits, which resemble those of the elm tree, with a middle seed surrounded by a thin, circular wing that enables the wind to carry them. Its common name refers to the fact that pioneers sometimes used the bitter fruit as a substitute for hops in flavoring beer. The hopbush belongs to the citrus family; the flowers and even the leaves, when crushed, exude a pleasant citrus odor. The plant grows from six to ten feet tall; its white flowers appear in April or May. Small native insects pollinate the flowers, and birds, such as flycatchers and phoebes, in turn eat the pollinators. The hopbush has three-parted glossy compound leaves with tiny teeth on their edges. The plant grows in canyon bottoms and shady areas of chaparral.
amh

Photo: © Br. Alfred Brousseau, Saint Mary's College

wild grape
Vitis californica

In autumn, the wild grape has bright, showy leaves of yellow and red as well as ripe purple fruit. The vine is especially common in riparian areas. Years ago when children did not spend so much time watching television, they would swing over creek beds by hanging onto wild grape vines. One grapevine can exceed 50 feet in length, becoming thick and woody at its base. Its tendrils allow it to grow over and through trees and shrubs. The leaves are maplelike, palmately veined into three lobes. Greenish-white flowers appear in early summer, and the edible purple grapes have developed by early autumn.
amh

the broken rope
of a tire swing—
wild grapes
            Linda Papanicolaou

Photos: Scott Hein (www.heinphoto.com) and
    J. E. (Jed) and Bonnie McClellan © California Academy of Sciences

WINTER

SKY AND ELEMENTS

cold rain

Cold rain—colder than snow. How the damp chill penetrates into our bones! Our legs and feet become soaked as the wind blows the rain beneath the erratic shelters of our umbrellas. The thermometer may not plummet as far as the numbers displayed across the national weather maps, but we feel that wet cold seeping throughout our being. And, as we watch the rain slide down the window pane, we are inclined toward melancholy and old memories. Cold rain epitomizes deep winter on the California coast. Often it evokes the ancient urge to gather by the fire and summon friends to share the warmth. We feel the cold rain so deeply and that in itself has meaning and its own kind of wintry beauty.
es

winter rain
a mouse runs
over the koto
        Buson

this cold rain blowing
from across the asphalt street
a neighbor's dim light
        Ebba Story

cold rain
the smells of wet woolen clothes
fill the hiking hut
        Joan Zimmerman

his deepening voice
reports he's just enlisted—
again cold rain, rain
        Carol Steele

Photo: Ted Homan (previous page), Tim Correia

LANDSCAPE

arroyos come alive

Some people believe that California has only two seasons —wet and dry. Very little, if any, rain falls in the San Francisco Bay Area from mid-May until mid-October. The little streams in the arroyos dry up during this time. In many areas winter is considered a season of quiet and waiting, but here the winter rains signal a time of rebirth, and the streambeds fill with the welcome sounds of flowing water. Little waterfalls appear here and there, especially where the streams run down the coastal cliffs into the ocean. Mosses on rocks that line the arroyos turn green. Near the end of winter, ferns send up their fiddleheads and, if the weather turns warm, some of our most delicate wildflowers bloom.
amh

Photo: Joseph Dougherty

kelp wrack

Underwater forests of bull kelp and giant kelp grow in favorable habitat along the coast of California. Winter storms uproot and break apart these huge algae and carry parts of them to the beaches. Wave action and the ebb and flow of the tides entangle the leaves, stipes and flotation bulbs of the kelp with other debris, forming large piles called wracks. The beached wracks provide shelter and food for a variety of life, including kelp flies and sand fleas. In turn these creatures provide food for the many shore birds that patrol the strand. When examined closely, kelp wracks provide a variety of interesting patterns.

Kelp does break free and individual stalks are washed ashore in most seasons, providing the fun of kelp bulb popping when the plant is mature. However, it is the winter occurrence of kelp wracks that is the most seasonal appearance of kelp on land.
pg/dcg

kelp wracks
finding the way around
with new friends
              D. Claire Gallagher
	morning-after friends
	tangled in feather boas
	plucked from kelp wrack
	              Joan Zimmerman

Photo: Patrick Gallagher

mudslides

Winter rains in California often bring mudslides that cause road closures and threaten homes, especially those in mountainous areas. Often late summer or early autumn wildfires denude the land of trees and shrubs that hold the soil with their roots. Late autumn rains typically saturate the ground. When the following winter rains are heavy, the ground no longer drains adequately. Groundwater comes to the surface, taking the surrounding earth with it, particularly in the wake of wildfires.

     Bay Area hillsides often show patches of depression, the results of slower mud slides that have oozed down like thick syrup. Below the slide, a tongue-like bulge appears. In natural areas, the slide kills everything in its path, tree or bushes for example, as their roots are inexorably torn out on their downhill ride. In inhabited areas, houses are sometimes destroyed by being drawn downhill by a slide. On small, backcountry roads, slides can creep down the roadsides onto the road surface. Navigating through the mud is like driving on ice.
amh

thank you,
god of mountains and mudslides
for this gentle rain
                Peggy Heinrich

Photo: Don Homan

snow on the peaks

The climate of the San Francisco Bay Area is so mild that snow on the ground in the cities and lower elevations where most people live is very rare. However, several times during most winters a storm that produces rain in the valleys deposits snow on the peaks of the mountains surrounding the Bay. When the storm clears, the next day's sunshine provides a view of the snow, sometimes only on a few peaks or occasionally across an entire ridge. The sight adds wonder to the realization that the storm has passed.
pg

Diablo's two peaks
lightly capped with white . . . but ah,
the snows of childhood
                      Anne M. Homan

snow on the peaks
lasts almost till noon—
this fast-paced life
                      Joan Zimmerman

Photo: Ted Homan

tule fog

In low-lying inland areas near San Francisco Bay, winter rains are often followed by a heavy ground fog. This fog is locally called tule fog. "Tule" is the Spanish/Aztec name for the bulrushes that grow in the bay and river margins where the fog appears.

     Tule fogs present a significant hazard to land and water travel. Aircraft landings are affected, and sometimes the fog is so persistent that travelers are marooned at the airports for days. Around the bay, mountain peaks and the tops of tall buildings are visible above the tule fog. From these highpoints the visible peaks appear to be an archipelago of green isles.

pg

a towhee skulks
under low junipers
tule fog
     Elaine and Neal Whitman

Photo: Ed Grossmith

HUMAN AFFAIRS

Julia Morgan

The anniversary of Julia Morgan's birth is January 20. She was born in 1872 in Oakland and continued to live there throughout her life. She graduated from Oakland High School and then from UC Berkeley in 1894 with a degree in civil engineering, the only woman in her class. She continued her studies at the L'École de Beaux Arts in Paris, France, where she earned her architectural certification at the age of 29. It was the first granted to a woman. In 1902 she returned to San Francisco and worked with an architectural firm; she opened her own practice two years later. She often worked in what is known today as the California Arts and Crafts style, an architectural style that emphasized simplicity and harmony with its surroundings. Phoebe Apperson Hearst persuaded Morgan to design buildings for the YWCA at Asilomar, a site on the coast near Pacific Grove. Morgan drew the plans and supervised the building of 16 structures; 13 are still at the site and are on the National Register of Historic Places. She designed a wide variety of buildings, from personal homes to churches to public buildings—almost 700 in all. She was also the estate architect for Hearst's Castle from 1919 to 1947, participating in planning and supervising the tiniest details. In 1951 she closed her office and spent much of her retirement in traveling to Europe and South America. She shunned publicity and said that her work should speak for itself. She died on February 2, 1957. The main repository of her work is the Julia Morgan Papers at Cal Poly; the Julia Morgan/Forney collection at Berkeley concentrates on her earliest years, from 1907 to 1917.
amh

    a collection of
beach cairns one of them for
    Julia Morgan
        Wendy Wright

Postcard: California Stage

olive harvest

The Olive Harvest Vase, now in the British Museum, was made in Italy about 520 BCE. It shows the same process of harvesting used today in the Mediterranean climate of the San Francisco Bay Area. Olives for oil are harvested here in early December and require a breakneck schedule, for olives must be processed within 24 hours of picking to achieve oil with high quality and flavor. Picking is mostly by hand or by swatting the trees with long poles or rakes—the cosmetic appearance of the fruit does not matter when it will be crushed to make oil. Occasionally, mechanical vibrating rakes are used. Harvesting nets spread on the ground collect the olives as they fall from the trees. A blower is used to separate the leaves, twigs and other detritus from the olives. Finally, the olives are loaded into wooden bins which are taken to an oil mill. About 80 pounds of olives can be harvested from a mature tree.

      The harvest for canning of whole olives begins earlier in the growing season. The olives are picked green for maximum firmness and require delicate handing to preserve their cosmetic appearance. These are all handpicked by workers who carefully remove the olives from the tree and place them in lug boxes or picking baskets.
amh

Olive harvest
workers share a loaf
of sour dough bread
                Garry Gay

Photo: Anne M. Homan

John Steinbeck

The anniversary of Steinbeck's death is December 20. He died at age 66 in 1968 in New York City. He was born in Salinas, California, and spent his early years there. A number of his short stories and novels are set in this area and the Monterey Peninsula. One of the best-known and most widely read American writers of the 20th century, Steinbeck received the Pulitzer Prize for *The Grapes of Wrath* in 1939. In 1962 he was awarded the Nobel Prize for Literature. Many of his works dealt with the lives of the working class and migrant workers during the Dust Bowl and the Great Depression. Seventeen of his works were transformed into films by Hollywood. The National Steinbeck Center in Salinas has an excellent presentation of the films as well as the restored Chevrolet camper-pickup named Rocinante that Steinbeck drove around the country while gathering material for *Travels with Charley*. The Steinbeck Center at San Jose has a large collection of his materials.
amh

ANIMALS

California newt
Taricha torosa torosa

California newts come out of hiding from December through January, depending on the winter rains. They head for ditches or stockponds and breed nearby; afterward the female attaches her clear jellylike egg mass to stones, roots or twigs in the water. The terrestrial adult ranges in color from a yellowish to dark brown above to pale yellow to orange below. The skin is sort of granular, slightly warty except during the breeding season when the male's skin becomes smoother. The iris of the eye is yellow. In size this newt ranges from three to ten inches. California newts eat earthworms, snails, slugs, sow bugs and insects. Their skin contains a potent neurotoxin, which keeps them safe from most predators. After the rainy season they are rarely seen because they retreat to cool, moist places underground, often in the burrows of ground squirrels.
amh

here
then not
newt
        Linda Papanicolaou

the glisten of newts
from a place in my childhood
damp morning after
        donnalynn chase
        Reeds, 2007

taricha torosa . . .
stumbles over rocks
in its lyric outfit
    Brenda Hillman
    from "Clouds near San Leandro"
    Pieces of Air in the Epic, 2005

Photo: Scott Hein (www.heinphoto.com)

elephant seal
Mirounga angustirostris

The northern elephant seal is named for the male's trunk-like proboscis and enormous size; the animal averages about 15 feet long and can weigh as much as 6,000 pounds. Females are about half as long and average about 2,000 pounds. Although hunted to the verge of extinction for oil by 1900, the elephant seal has made a good comeback and now has a population estimated at 120,000. Breeding sites range from Guadalupe Island off the Baja coast up to the Farallon Islands. The largest mainland rookery is at Año Nuevo, a low, windswept point about 55 miles south of San Francisco, now a state park. Male seals arrive there from early December through January; pregnant females come to give birth from late December through early February. The males fight on the beach to keep and protect their harems, often leaving the loser bloodied. Richard Cole said in his article on elephant seals for *Marine Mammal News* that visitors on guided tours in the park can sometimes "watch the awesome spectacle of a two-ton bull slashing the chest of a harem-raiding male rival while emitting guttural roars sounding like a rapid-fire foghorn." The winner of the fight is called the alpha bull or beachmaster. Adult elephant seals are varying shades of brown or black. The black pups, born in the sand dunes, make dog-like yelping noises and nurse for about a month. After the pups are born, the adults mate on land. Gradually, they return to the ocean, where they spend 80 per cent of their lives. During the nonbreeding season, the animals range up to Alaska. Although awkward on land with its bulk and small limbs, the elephant seal is graceful and at home in the ocean. It can dive down a mile and spend as much as two hours underwater foraging for fish and squid.
amh

no beach blankets . . .
rows of elephant seals doze,
flip sand
          Deborah P. Kolodji

Photo: Scott Hein (www.heinphoto.com)

junco flocks
Junco hyemalis

In the winter many birds aggregate into flocks. The junco feeds and flies in mixed flocks with sparrows, often seemingly swept along with leaves by the north wind at a wood's edge. The flocks return to the same area each winter. White outer tail feathers make the junco stand out in flight from its sparrow companions. Although the junco is found in the Bay Area all year, the gathering of flocks makes the bird more prominent in winter. All juncos have a black head and neck, forming a sort of hood. The western Oregon form has a rusty back with a whitish belly. The birds feed mostly on the ground, eating weed and grass seeds. About the same size as a sparrow, the junco will eat seeds from a feeder on the ground or on trays. The junco's song is a short trill or series of trills, usually on one pitch. amh

a junco flock
grazing on the hill
the Twenty-Third Psalm
        Elaine and Neal Whitman

Photo: Kim Cabrera

ladybug, lady beetle, ladybird
Hippodamia convergens

kigo: migrating ladybugs (winter), departing ladybugs (spring), lady bug (spring)

During the late autumn, California ladybugs, really lady beetles, begin their migration to over-wintering sites. The reddish-orange beetles with twelve black spots gather in large hibernating aggregations that are often hidden in leaf litter and plant crevices. Their traditional migration to the Sierra started after the Central Valley and its supply of aphids dried up in the late summer. Today, with the advent of irrigation in the Valley, the migration can take place later and the wind currents blow some of the beetles to the Coastal Mountains. In the mild Bay Area climate the aggregations may be more exposed to view. Hikers in the winter might see them in a clearing near a stream or even occasionally washed up on beaches. Collectors, mindful of the ladybug's use for control of aphids in our gardens, gather the beetles from December through February, cold store them and sell them for release in the spring. A ladybug larva can consume an average of 50 aphids per day; an adult, 22 aphids.

     Ladybugs have captured our attention and affection for centuries. In Europe long, long ago the "Beetle of Our Lady" was dedicated to the Virgin Mary; in the U.S. at least seven states have adopted one of the 450 species of native lady beetles as a state insect. It is one of the few insects that enchant most children, who allow the brightly colored animal to crawl on their hands and recite the old nursery rhyme: "Ladybug, ladybug, fly away home …"
DCG

ladybug sky
the sting of their wings
against my cheekbones
          Alison Woolpert

some with spots
this one without—is it sir
or madame ladybug
          Alison Woolpert

inner centering
on a hazy afternoon—
smack...ladybug swarm
          Judith Schallberger

sitting here searching
ladybug walks on my words
I think she's winking
          Toni Homan
          YTHS anthology 2009

Photo: Patrick Gallagher

northern harrier
Circus cyaneus

      The northern harrier migrates to the San Francisco Bay Area in the winter from its breeding grounds in Canada and Alaska. The name "circus," meaning "ring" comes from the distinctive white ring band of its rump, visible from above the bird while it is in flight. A popular nickname for it is the cigar-band hawk. The bird averages about 20 inches long; its wingspread about 43 inches. The males are gray-backed, but the females and juveniles are brown. The old name for this species was the "marsh hawk" because of its hunting habit of coursing back and forth, flying low over open fields or marshes, its wings in a V-shape, listening for small birds or rodents. Small birds which try to attack can be caught by the harrier's flipping upside down in flight and impaling the bird's soft belly with its talons. amh

northern harrier
with a twitch of a feather
skims the wild grasses
                Anne M. Homan

sanderling
Calidris alba

The sanderling winters in flocks on Bay Area beaches, coming from its breeding ground in the high Arctic, far away from the world's popular watering spots. This small sandpiper is about 6 inches tall, with a black bill and black feet. It has pale gray plumage above and white below in the winter. In flight its bold white wing-stripes are noticeable. With quick, little steps the flock follows the tide line, running ahead of the incoming wave, then turning around and running after the receding wave to snap up stranded invertebrates or probe in the wet sand for a tasty morsel.
amh

beach mosaic
left by sanderlings
my footprints now, too
        Deborah P. Kolodji

wind chop—
sanderlings feed
on the edge of the surge
        Linda Papanicolaou

Photo: Bon Terra Consulting

steelhead
Oncorhynchus mykiss

The sea-run rainbow trout or steelhead travels up freshwater rivers and streams to spawn in winter after rains have filled the water courses. The steelhead is the same species as the freshwater rainbow trout, but like the salmon, it lives in the ocean until it returns to spawn in its original hatching ground in fresh water. Unfortunately, the urbanization of the San Francisco Bay Area has interfered with this practice, and few steelhead make their way very far upstream. Much reduced from historic numbers, they still survive in altered streams and polluted water, a tribute to their tenacity of life. Current efforts are underway in many areas to remove unnecessary dams, open up concrete channels and control pollution to protect and restore the fishery. Steelhead were caught with weir and spear by native Ohlones and were an important food source for them. Steelhead are often pursued by sea lions, who lie in wait for them at river mouths and adjacent beaches. The steelhead can grow to 36 pounds but averages about 10 pounds. It is silvery, with a steel blue coloration above the lateral line when at sea. In freshwater it becomes a silvery-green with black spots. For stream fisherman, there are few more exciting game fish than the steelhead.
ra

Photo: Jerry Smith

white-crowned sparrow
Zonotrichia leucophrys

Another winter visitor from Alaska to the Bay Area is the white-crowned sparrow. Its bright black and white striped head, yellowish-pink bill, gray breast and the usual sparrow mixture of brownish/black/white feathers on its back give it a handsome, well-dressed look. In the winter this sparrow often travels in flocks, scattering through low bushes and thickets and hopping in fields and gardens, foraging for insects and seeds of weeds, grasses and grain. On the ground they often search with a "double-scratch"—this involves a quick hop backwards to turn over leaves followed by a forward hop and pounce.
amh

winter feeder guest—
the white-crowned sparrow's
O sweet Canada
                Linda Papanicolaou

Photo: Alden M. Johnson © California Academy of Sciences

yellow-billed magpie
Pici nuttalli

The large dome-shaped nests of the magpie, built of sticks and mud, are easily visible in the winter, high in a sycamore, cottonwood or oak tree. Mostly in the winter magpies make shallow pits in the ground to cache food. Three requirements are necessary for magpies to flourish—a stream, a grove of tall trees and grassland. The yellow-billed magpie is found only in California, mostly in the San Joaquin Valley, spreading westward into some smaller valleys, such as the Livermore Valley. It has a yellow bill and a yellow stripe that surrounds its eyes. The body is white and iridescent black with a very long tail. It is omnivorous, eating insects, earthworms, acorns, fruit and carrion. They nest in small colonies and are very gregarious with their whining calls of "maag" and a series of "chucks." The magpie population was seriously depleted in the 1920s and 1930s with ground squirrel poisoning, which also affected their main summer food source—grasshoppers. A new threat is the West Nile Virus, which has killed thousands of them.
amh

four lane blacktop—
a magpie on a fencepost
watching the trucks
           Linda Papanicolaou

Photo: Richard Finn

PLANTS

artichoke
Cynara scolymus

kigo: artichoke (spring); Artichoke Festival (spring); frost-nipped artichoke or frost-tipped artichoke (winter)

The artichoke, a perennial that grows three or four feet tall and six feet in diameter, is in the thistle family. Because of its long, slender, silvery-green leaves, it resembles a fern. The fruit is a globe covered with spiny leaves surrounding the heart and a fuzzy choke. If this flowerbud is allowed to remain unpicked, it will produce a beautiful violet flower about six to seven inches across.

Although there are about 50 varieties of artichoke worldwide, only the *Green Globe* or Italian variety, is grown commercially in the U.S. and most of them are grown within a five-mile radius of Castroville, CA, known as the Artichoke Capitol of the World. Artichokes seem to enjoy the sandy soil and the moderate temperatures of the coast. Artichokes are planted, cultivated, and harvested by hand so you see workers in the fields in all seasons. The peak season for artichokes is late March through May although they produce all year round. However, farmers usually cut back the plants in the summer to ensure a better crop in the fall and winter. Some winters there might be a mild frost and the tips of the artichoke turn a bluish-silvery black. There are those who think that the frost-nipped artichoke is the crème de la crème of artichoke eating. It's worth noting that during the Renaissance, especially in France, artichokes were considered an aphrodisiac.

Castroville hosts the Artichoke Festival every year in May celebrating the artichoke with booths and food and crowning of the Artichoke Queen. The chosen queen is in good company as one of the earliest to be crowned was a Hollywood unknown, Marilyn Monroe. It was 1948 and she was on the verge of stardom.
pjm

Artichoke Festival—
a young Norma Jean queen
before her time
        pjm

from across the room
you can tell they are lovers—
frost-nipped artichoke
        pjm

Photo: Anne M. Homan

coyote brush
Baccharis pilularis

As the tiny seeds of coyote brush mature, the spent flowers burst and release silky gossamer threads to the breeze. By early December the prolific white silk has been driven by the wind into drifts and low mats that from a distance look like snow. At night it reflects back the moon. For weeks, the silk billows through the air and sticks to anything in its path. Most winters this provides the appearance of Currier and Ives without the cold.

      Coyote brush is our most common native shrub. Its many branches bear small, leathery, sometimes toothed leaves that are resinous and become fragrant on hot days. Although a modest plant, rarely reaching its ten-foot maximum height, coyote brush is conspicuous in several ways. An evergreen, it stands out in the chaparral when other plants are brown in the dry heat. The dense growth, so difficult to penetrate, inspired Native Americans on the coast to name it for Coyote, an anthropomorphic spirit with great ingenuity. New plants spread easily even on bare ground in shallow rocky soil; it is invasive and aggressive, frequently colonizing unkempt land as a "pioneer" shrub.

This species has separate male and female plants; the small flower heads of both are without rays. The differences in form and shading of the bloom make it possible to determine the sex of the bush. Coyote brush is a late bloomer—in September to November after other plants have died back. The female's white flowers are like miniature shaving brushes.

dcg

soft down of coyote brush
I open my palm
              to the wind
                    Laurie Stoelting

Photo: Rebecca Davies

oak mistletoe
Phoradendron villosum

Winter is the time when mistletoe is most visible in the Bay Area. Its large, shrubby masses remain concealed high off the ground until the deciduous oaks lose their leaves. Native black walnut trees are also susceptible to the hemi-parasite. Even though mistletoe has green leaves and stems and can photosynthesize, the plant is dependent on its tree host for needed water and minerals. The name "Phoradendron" means "thief of the tree" in Greek. In the evolutionary process, mistletoe lost its roots, so it penetrates tree bark to gain access to what it cannot provide itself. The mistletoe's thick, leathery leaves are arranged in opposite pairs on woody twigs. The plant blooms all year with minute, green wind-pollinated flowers; the berries that follow are white or sometimes pinkish. Birds love the sticky berries. As they feed, they scrape their beaks against nearby branches, trying to rub away the sticky residue, thus spreading the parasite.

    Mistletoe was the sacred plant of the Druids in England. They believed that mistletoe had special powers to cure diseases and to keep evil away. Before the Christmas tree became customary, English families created a globe made of greenery with holly and ivy, ribbons, apples, candles and some mistletoe. This globe was hung somewhere from a ceiling in the house, and the idea of catching people to kiss beneath it began. Then it was called a "kissing bough."

amh

in the tree branches
mistletoe against the sky
a small cloud floats by
           Kiyoko Tokutomi

Photo: Don Homan

sycamore
Platanus racemosa

The western, or California, sycamore stands out in the winter, with its one-inch seed balls still hanging on bare branches. With its leaves gone, the tree's distinctive flaking bark is exposed—a puzzle-like patchwork of light brown, gray and cream. Our native sycamore often has a recumbent growth along the arroyos, unlike the stiffly-standing nonnative sycamores used for shade trees along the street of our cities. Mature trees stand from 30 to 90 feet high. Like the bigleaf maple, the sycamore inhabits the Bay Area's riparian woodlands and canyon bottoms. And like the maple, it has large toothed palmate leaves. Birds love the seeds and help break open the balls to the wind for distribution. Water-loving animals such as the raccoon and wood duck often find cavities in the trunk and branches for homes. One of the oldest and largest stands of the tree is at Sycamore Grove Park near Livermore.
amh

his depression
seeing it as it really is—
leafless sycamore
    donnalynn chase

Old sycamore
raccoon eyes stare at me
from a hollow space
    Garry Gay

Photo: Anne M. Homan

toyon
Heteromeles arbutifolia

An evergreen shrub or small tree native to the chaparral and dry wooded foothills, toyon bears prodigious clusters of red berries in the winter. This festive bounty and the glossy toothed leaves inspired the common names Christmas berry and California holly. It is thought that masses of this shrub growing in the hills above the present-day Hollywood gave the community its name. Both the Indians and the Spanish Californios considered the sweet spicy berries to be a treat; flocks of wintering birds still do. Toyon's bright green leaves and brilliant berries color the short days of California winter.
dcg

such a fuss
as though nothing lasts
birds, toyon berries
            Roger Abe

twinkle of sunlight
in the toyon berries—
our train clatters on
            Ebba Story

Photo: Patrick Gallagher

www.ingramcontent.com/pod-product-compliance
Lightning Source LLC
Chambersburg PA
CBHW041832300426

44111CB00002B/59